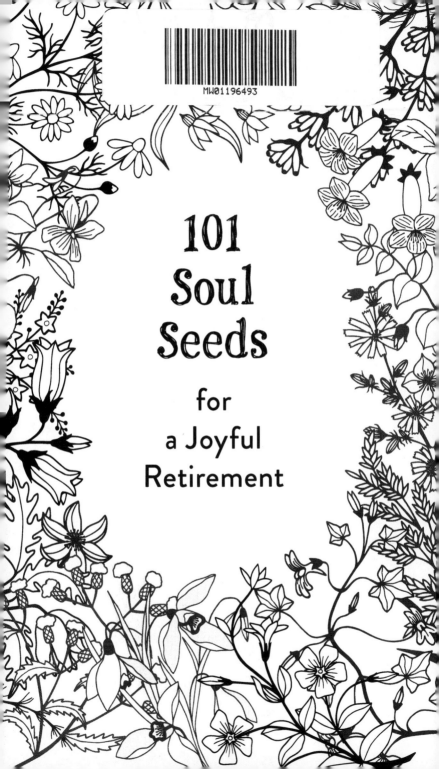

101
Soul
Seeds

for
a Joyful
Retirement

Anamchara
Books

Vestal, New York 13850
www.AnamcharaBooks.com

Paperback ISBN: 978-1-62524-842-8
eBook ISBN: 978-1-62524-843-5

Cover design and interior layout by Micaela Grace.
Plant drawings by 999041 | Dreamstime.com.

101
Soul Seeds

for a Joyful Retirement

BRUCE G. EPPERLY

RETIREMENT AS CHALLENGE, VOCATION, AND ADVENTURE

My call to retirement from full-time pastoral ministry came unexpectedly. When my son and his family moved to Cape Cod to be near us in 2014, we had a tacit agreement that if he needed to return to Washington, DC, to run his DC-based business, my wife and I would return as well. So in 2021, as the pandemic began to subside, he began to hint that he and his family would be returning to our nation's capital.

Initially, I was gobsmacked, to say the least. Although at sixty-eight I was of retirement age and receiving both Medicare and Social Security, I still felt I had many productive years ahead of me as Senior Pastor of South Congregational Church, United Church of Christ, located in Centerville, one of the seven villages of Barnstable, Massachusetts, just a short walk from the Nantucket Sound. Although I had already served as pastor of this historic congregation for eight years, I was hoping to serve till my seventieth and possibly even seventy-fifth birthday.

Although we were "wash-ashores," that is, new-comers to Cape Cod, this beautiful and fragile peninsula of beaches, sand dunes, osprey, piping plovers, right whales, and quaint historic villages had become our home. I was a daily beachcomber, walking the sandy paths of Craigville, Covell's, and Long beaches for an hour every morning, rain or shine, snow or sun, gusty or calm. My wife Kate and I anticipated aging in place on the Cape.

I loved my work as a village pastor, leading a congregation that appreciated my gifts as a writer and teacher and the integration of scholarship, spirituality, mysticism, and social concern that characterized my preaching and ministry. I would miss the community, the folks in our church and neighborhood. I delighted in being a village pastor, well-known in the community and recognized on my morning walks, where I had been described as "mayor of the beach."

With each passing day, the possibility of retirement became more concrete as our son and daughter-in-law put their home up for sale, received an offer the first week, and then purchased a home in Bethesda, Maryland, just a mile from where my wife and I had lived twenty years earlier. The reality of retirement continued to hit home as I announced my departure to the congregation, and then began the process of selling our home and leading the church in preparing for the next steps in its 225-year adventure.

Like preparing for weddings and funerals, the busyness of moving is both emotionally stressful and beneficial. For a brief time, you are focused on the task at hand and don't have time to think about the significant personal, professional, and emotional changes—gains and losses—that lie ahead. As we prepared to move, there never seemed to be enough hours in the day to dwell on the realities of change, as we spent our time getting the house ready for the showing, evaluating offers, and then beginning the arduous and sometimes sentimental process involved in selling or disposing of nearly half of our possessions, including over two thousand books from my home and church offices. Lunches and dinners with friends and congregants were bittersweet—celebrative yet filled with anticipatory grief and the unspoken possibility that we might never meet again.

For many of us in the Western world, retirement is one of life's "necessary losses," to use the phrase coined by author and researcher Judith Viorst. If we live long enough and have enough largesse, eventually we will let go of the work that defined much of our lives for decades. We will have to imagine and then embark on new adventures, exploring the contours of new identities and vocations and finding new ways to pass the time and create novel futures, filled with hope, meaning, and joy.

During the first months of preparation for retirement as well as its initial months, I took solace in the adventures of the biblical patriarch and matriarch Abraham and Sarah, called forth in their seventies from their beloved home in Haran to sojourn across a barely charted wilderness in quest of a promised land. I pondered their practice of setting up altars as they went forth by stages toward an unfamiliar future. I realized that I needed to create my own spiritual and vocational altars to mark out the geography of retirement. Looking toward the interplay of gain and loss, characteristic of retirement, I also was inspired by God's promise to the prophet Jeremiah:

> For surely I know the plans I have for you . . . plans for your welfare and not for harm, to give you a future with hope. Then when you call upon me and come and pray to me, I will hear you. When you search for me, you will find me;

if you seek me with all your heart, I will let you find me and restore your fortunes. (Jeremiah 29:11–14)

As I contemplated God's words to an anxious prophet, I experienced my own sense that God was with me, guiding my steps and providing an open future, filled with possibilities, even though I was as yet unaware of them. God desires me—and everyone else—to prosper in our unique contexts and life situations. God also invites me in the concrete limitations of my life to be the agent and artist of my own destiny. Like the "Choose Your Own Adventure" books I read over thirty years ago with my son Matt when he was in elementary school, I have many choices in retirement and each choice will lead me down a pathway filled with adventures, possibilities, and pitfalls. I realized that God makes a way forward where I see dead ends, and that in envisioning a far horizon filled with possibilities, I will be creating my future in partnership with God. I will be a companion, if I choose, in God's quest to heal the world, regardless of my professional or personal status.

The Great Jubilee

In early 2019, I attended a conference at the Louisville Institute for recipients of the Institute's Pastoral Study Grants. As I shared my project on clergy retirement, one of the participants surprised me when she stated that the word for retirement is "jubilee" in Spanish. I queried my dear friend Edwin David Aponte, director of the Louisville Institute, and he noted, "Yes, *jubilación* is the word for retirement." Imagine that—retirement as a time for jubilation. Imagine your retirement as a jubilee, the celebration of an important event in your life, an end of one journey and the beginning of a new pilgrimage. This interchange inspired the title of my book on clergy retirement, *The Jubilee Years: Embracing Clergy Retirement* (published by Rowman and Little-field). When the book went into print in November 2020, little did I know that I would be embracing my own first steps toward retirement in less than three months!

I believe that retirement is an invitation to embark on a holy adventure. The process of retirement involves the interplay of subtraction and addition. A time of simplifying to be open to new things as a prelude to abundant life. Retirement is also a season of "lasts" and "firsts." As I look toward retirement from full-time ministry, I consider all the daily and weekly activities for which I will no longer be responsible: daily morning prayer services on Zoom during the pandemic, weekly worship and preaching, agendas for board meetings, community relations, budget preparation, hospital calls and pastoral care, and staff supervision. I must say goodbye to these and claim the finality of jettisoning certain responsibilities that have characterized my daily life for decades. While I found meaning in all these activities, I will no longer plan my days around them. I will still care but I will no longer have responsibility, and I will have to practice appropriate boundaries with former congregants. From now on, I will have to let others counsel the troubled, care for the sick, comfort the bereaved, and companion the dying of my beloved flock.

There will be many "firsts": days without necessary appointments or unexpected pastoral calls, worship and sermon planning, morning prayer services and study groups. In the wide-open schedules of retirement, I can choose how I spend my days and have opportunities to call a friend to get together spontaneously. I doubt that I will sleep in, since I enjoy getting up for meditation, study, and walking at 4:30 a.m. I still delight in writing. But I can happily take an afternoon nap without worrying about missing a meeting or finishing my next sermon. I will no longer need to set my Alexa alarm to remind me of classes and appointments as I did during the COVID pandemic. There will be "firsts" as well in terms of involvement in a congregation as a member and not pastor, volunteer activities at church and in the community, and classes and sermons as a guest and not a settled leader. Although we spent twenty years in the US capital, I will need to learn new routes for my morning walks, reconnect with old friends, and reach out to new friends.

Yes, retirement can be a jubilee, filled with hopeful adventures and meaningful projects. We can experience jubilation with time for post-COVID travel, leisurely lunches, new projects, and extra time for volunteer work and political involvement. We can choose to be "good ancestors," actively participating in God's vision of Shalom and working to ensure a healthy future for our grandchildren and future generations. We can take up a new avocation or consult, without time or financial constraints, inspired by our gifts and passions.

The Soul Seeds of Retirement

I am a writer. I try to write a few pages every morning. Often when I want to understand something more fully or work through an issue, I take to my study and computer, joining research, experience, thought, and emotion to forge guideposts for the next steps of my journey. This book is the fruit of my ruminations in the months when I was announcing my retirement, moving, and then settling in a new home. Writing a soul seed each day helped me orient myself to the adventure ahead, enabling me to come to terms with the reality of change and imagine the great "What's next?" in my life, professional interests, marriage, and relationships with family and friends.

Although I am new to retirement, I wrote these soul seeds to embrace the questions retirement brings as well as to find the vague outlines of answers I will need to live into so I can experience joy and meaning in my own retirement. The meaning of the soul seeds for the future changed as I progressed in my retirement journey. I am still figuring out the landscape of retirement, and I doubt I will ever fully comprehend the possibilities of retirement for personal, vocational, and spiritual growth. That ignorance and incompleteness are good, for the best life always embraces the unknown and unfinished.

I also wrote these reflections as a gift to persons like yourself who are retired or preparing for retirement so that you may experience retirement as a joyful jubilee, in which you can live more expansively, making a difference in new and creative ways. We are pilgrims, but we are not strangers. We are on a common journey, though our routes and responsibilities may differ.

Questions and Possibilities

Retirement is filled with questions, few of which are immediately answered. Challenging as these questions may be, we may learn, with the poet Rilke, to love the questions and see them as invitations to spiritual adventure and self-discovery. In that spirit, each soul seed will conclude with questions for reflection, an opportunity to reflect more deeply on some aspect of the spiritual adventure of retirement. The soul seeds and questions are intentionally concrete. I believe that spirituality is lived out in the challenges, ambiguities, and duties of everyday life and not in a blissful eternity. Our character is formed by our deepest beliefs, and our deepest beliefs are refined in the crucible of family and professional life, citizenship, and eventually aging and retirement.

As you begin to ponder retirement, or are already retired and looking for direction, here are some questions to begin your reflections. Take time for quiet reflection, fantasizing, or imaginative visualization. After all, there's no hurry, is there?

What are your images of retirement?

What dreams will lure you forward and get you up each morning?

What obligations await you in retirement? (Yes, there may be obligations, such as our hands-on care for our grandchildren who will be nine and eleven when I retire.)

What new projects will excite your passions?

What concerns do you have about retirement?

How will retirement change your relationships with friends, children, and life partners?

What gifts will emerge to respond to the needs of those around you?

If you enjoy journaling, you might jot down some insights. If you like music or artistry, you might write a song or poem, or draw your visions of retirement.

Retirement does not mean passivity or sitting on life's sidelines. You are an agent of your destiny and the artist of your experience. You can "choose your own adventure." You can discover the fullness of simplicity and the energy of the aging process. You may discover deeper passions that you had not previously imagined. Roads not taken may emerge, and gifts undiscovered may be mined. Your retirement may be the pilgrimage on your own Camino de Santiago, a pilgrimage of faith, even if it is a journey without distance, stretching far into the future and lived out one unrepeatable day at a time on your holy adventure with God and loved ones as your companions.

Wisdom from Many Voices

This book is intended to be an inspiration for personal reflection. I encourage you to see these 101 soul seeds as a spur to intellectual, spiritual, and vocational adventure. If you are able, set aside time for silence, breathing deeply the interplay of past, present, and future; embracing with gratitude the gifts of others in your personal journey; and seeing these gifts as catalysts for the journey ahead. With God as your companion, let gratitude and hope guide your way.

In my first three contributions to the "101 Soul Seeds" series (*101 Soul Seeds for Grandparents Working for a Better World*, *101 Soul Seeds for Peacemakers and Justice Seekers*, and *101 Soul Seeds for Healing and Wholeness*, all published by Anamchara Books), I began each contemplative entry with a saying from a noted spiritual guide, theologian, philosopher, physician, or artist. I have taken a slightly different turn in this book, quoting instead spiritual and cultural creatives in religion, philosophy, and the arts, ranging from the Bible and Plato to Maya Angelou and Thich Nhat Hanh. I also chose to include insightful comments from members of my James Lick High School Class of 1970. We missed our fiftieth reunion in 2020 due to the COVID pandemic, but in the process of planning and then canceling the reunion, I reconnected with many of my classmates, the majority of whom are retired and exploring new possibilities for the next decades of their lives. I queried a dozen of my classmates with questions such as, "What gives you purpose and meaning in retirement? What gets you up in the morning? What counsel do you have for other retirees?" The answers I received and the conversations I had were illuminating. My classmates had lived interesting and challenging lives and had grown through the process. They were now looking forward to new adventures of creativity and service. After decades apart, we had become friends again and would stay in touch as our futures unfold.

If the Spirit speaks to us in "sighs too deep for words" (Romans 8:26), then the Spirit must be speaking in Her own unique way in the lives of my classmates—sometimes in words, other times in synchronous encounters, images, poetry, and friendships. I included their words as a witness that no one is "ordinary" and that each of us has wisdom to share with our neighbors.

You may think that your journey is ordinary, but I believe your life is unique in challenge and possibility. The words I've said for years to the children of our church apply to you as you reflect on your retirement: "God loves you. You matter. You can do something great and wonderful with your life." As you hear the voices of my classmates, as well as artists and sages, let their words be an inspiration to listen to your own inner wisdom, to the voice of the Spirit whispering to you in the contours of your own unique and wild and precious life. Trust that God will provide for your deepest needs and that Spirit is inspiring you each new day. Rejoice in the Jubilee Years!

1.

For all that has been—thanks!

—DAG HAMMARSKJOLD

O n the day of our open house, when prospective buyers were due to tour our home, my wife purchased a new doormat to greet them with the words *Thankful. Grateful. Blessed.* This affirmation captures the jubilant spirit of joyful retirement—and as the German mystic Meister Eckhardt once noted, if the only prayer you make is "thank you," that will be enough. Today, let us give thanks for what has been—both the successes and failures that have led to this moment in time. When we give thanks, we recognize

all the people who supported our journey, as well as our own achievements. We remember God's presence, providing possibilities, inspirations, and challenges. We experience the graceful interdependence of life, which shaped our journey from our conception to this moment in time. With a thankful spirit, we can embrace the changes to come—in vocation and avocation, schedules and unplanned time, relationships and solitude, and health and wisdom. Each day will be filled with delight in another day of living.

Take a moment today to look at your life journey. For what are you grateful? For whom are you thankful? What pivotal events brought you to this moment in time?

**Holy One, thank You for the gift of life.
Thank You for waking me up today to another day of wonder, beauty, and possibility.**

2.

For all that shall be—yes!

—DAG HAMMARSKJOLD

Retirement ushers in the great "what's next?" Many questions surface: How will I spend this time of my life? What will get me up in the morning with joy and passion? What will give me hope as I look to the future? Where will I use the gifts and talents that shaped my working life, and what new gifts and talents will I explore? After years of writing serious academic works, many of my friends have turned to writing fiction and poetry. They want to use their minds in retirement but now choose to investigate

the more right-brain, poetic side of their personalities. Other friends who have been intellectual elites are now turning to woodworking, bluegrass music, garage bands, and gardening. Still other friends who have worked in trades such as carpentry and plumbing are now pursuing poetry, painting, bird-watching, and tutoring.

What is your great "yes"? What visions lead you forward? Finding the new possibilities in your future can bring joy and hope to every day.

Creative Spirit, inspire my own creativity.
Reveal my gifts of creativity, service,
and relationship to give hope to the world
around me.

3.

Be mindful of the second leg.

—KATE EPPERLY

A friend sprained her ankle while putting on her pants one morning. Standing on one foot as she attempted to pull up the second leg, she fell over, much to her pain and embarrassment. As my wife reflected on our friend's mishap, she noted, "Retirement is really the second leg of life." Putting on this second leg of life requires awareness of our limitations as well as our possibilities, the risks we face as well as the rewards. New possibilities emerge during this time of our lives, and so do novel pitfalls. We can't afford to be

careless with our lives in retirement—but taking care doesn't mean living small or anxiously. Care-filled living asks that we take responsibility for our emotional, intellectual, relational, and physical well-being, so we can make a difference in the world in the years ahead. With Divine help, we can put on retirement's "second leg," "renewing our strength, mounting up with wings like eagles, running and not being weary, and walking and not fainting" (Isaiah 40:31, author's paraphrase). Limitation—the concreteness of life—can be the womb of possibility.

What limitations do you face today? What limitations do you anticipate in the years ahead? Can you see the potential for possibility in these limitations?

Wisdom of the Universe, remind me to be mindful of my life's wondrous possibilities as well as its risks.

4.

Remember the first rule of the
wilderness—don't panic.

—MARY PIPHER

I must make a confession: When I am driving and find myself lost or my gas gauge suddenly blinks, my tendency is to speed up. I don't know where I'm going, and I know that driving faster burns up more fuel, but I just want to get somewhere—and quick. I want to get out of this mess, regardless of the consequences. Most of the time, however, I pause a moment and don't act on my first impulse. I slow down, or I stop and take a breath, look at my surroundings, recognizing that to

get to my destination, I need to know where I am. I need to be still and open to Divine wisdom.

What do you notice in stillness? What wisdom comes when you truly listen to your deepest inclinations or journal your experiences? One of the most important pathways to wise aging is simply pausing and looking at your current life situation. Contrary to the popular adage, "Don't stand there, do something," doing nothing may be the best response to post-retirement confusion or anxiety. Let go of your desire for performance and productivity; discern where you are and what next steps will deepen your spirit and give direction to your new adventure.

God of the Journey, teach me the gift of non-doing. Let me take time to discern the pathway of wisdom.

5.

The one who began a good
work in you will bring it
to completion by the day of Jesus Christ . . .
that your love my overflow more
and more with knowledge
and full insight to determine what is best . . .
having produced a harvest of righteousness.

—PHILIPPIANS 3:3–11 (EXCERPTS)

Retirement is a time of harvest. A time in which a lifetime of growth, integrity, and learning comes to fruition. The Divine aim at beauty, growth, and innovation doesn't stop when you turn in your keys

and receive your first pension check. God still has a vision for you and is providing you with the energy to achieve it. From the moment of your conception, God's love took form in your cells and your soul and will continue to do so in the future. The work the Spirit began in your life continues on.

Visualize your own personal harvest. What does it look like? How will it nourish your neighbors? What practices do you need to cultivate now to make your harvest fruitful?

Bless the path I am on, Spirit of God, and inspire me to be part of Your creative work, adding to the joy and beauty of the world.

6.

A self is not something static,
tied up in a pretty parcel
and handed to the child, finished and complete.
A self is always becoming.

—MADELEINE L'ENGLE

According to the Gospels, Jesus grew in wisdom and stature—and so can we. A living self is a growing self. Life is never complete. New possibilities are emerging with each new moment and day. We can choose to go beyond past achievements. We can learn new skills. We can deepen our spirituality through prayer and meditation, and widen our

horizons through education and travel. God does new things to match changes in our environment. God calls and we respond, and in response to us, God explores new potential for Divine action in the world. New ideas and possibilities are constantly flowing into our lives.

Where do you see yourself growing in the future? What new routes will you take in the artistry of life?

Artist of the Universe, awaken me to abundant possibilities. Let my imagination and agency break down self-imposed barriers, and let my life bring joy to myself and to the world.

7.

My seventies were interesting, and fairly serene,
but my eighties are passionate.
I grow more intense as I age.

—FLORIDA SCOTT-MAXWELL

A Divine Passion flows through life. It is the passion of the arc of the universe, aiming toward justice and beauty. It flows through all creation, and it flows through you. To the world, you may appear placid—but deep within you a fire may be brightly burning: a fire of compassion for the marginalized and forgotten; a flame of justice for the oppressed and mistreated; embers of hope for an end to war; and sparks ascend-

ing to illumine the paths of others. Let your inner fire warm, agitate, and illuminate, joining with others' fires to enlighten the world.

Where is your deepest passion? Where do you see fire in your life? How might you let the fire out in ways that bring warmth and healing to the world?

May the flames of the Spirit burst forth in me to enlighten and enliven the world.

8.

The place God calls you to is the place
where your deep gladness and the
world's deep hunger meet.

—FREDERICK BUECHNER

What is your deep gladness? What gets you up in the morning and excites your spirit? What do you look forward to at the end of the day? There is a synchronicity between our gifts and the world's needs. Even apparently random encounters—an article on page four of your local newspaper, a segment on cable news, a chance meeting, or an event in your community—can be God seeking to awaken you to the

congruence of your gifts and the world's needs. There are "burning bushes" on every thoroughfare. Hidden beneath every street sign is "Damascus Road" and the possibility of a mystical encounter. Listen to your life—your gifts, talents, and dreams—and listen to the voice of God speaking through the world around you. What signals are you receiving? What yearnings are waiting to be fulfilled in your life? Where does your deep gladness offer sustenance to the world's deep hunger?

Holy Imagination, awaken me to my deep gladness and attune me to the world's needs.

9.

Don't ask what the world needs.
Ask what makes you come alive, and go do it.
Because what the world needs is
people who have come alive.

—HOWARD THURMAN

Retirement may involve strategic withdrawals from social and political involvement. We may need time to recover from forty years of hard work. We don't need to feel guilty about going on vacation or taking up golf, pickleball, or tennis. Time spent painting, writing, and hiking may be balm for our souls. In retirement's yin and yang, contemplation balanced

with action, we need times of delight and rest, times when we can also listen to our deep passions, allowing them to illumine, energize, and empower us. Then, restored in mind, body, and spirit, we can put our passions to work in transforming our relationships and the world.

What burns deeply in your soul? What is unfinished, undiscovered, and waiting to come alive?

God of infinite passion, open my spirit to my deepest passions that I may set the world on fire with Your loving justice.

10.

Service is the rent we pay for being.
It is the very purpose of life, and not something
you do in your spare time.

—MARIAN WRIGHT EDELMAN

Our lives can be insulated and isolated, self-inter-
ested, acting solely for our own benefit. Or we
can see our retirement lives filled with opportunities
for service and mission. We can devote every moment,
even on the golf course or at supper with friends, to
adding beauty and joy to the world. We can explore
ways in which we can support the well-being of our
community by simple and unheralded acts of inten-

tional kindness. We can aspire to make every encounter a prayer and every act a blessing. We are part of an intricate and graceful tapestry of interdependence. Each of our actions sends ripples across the universe as well as our neighborhood.

Where are you called to serve? How can you transform every day into encounters of blessing?

Help me, O Spirit, to see You in every face and nurture You in every encounter.

11.

I coach to make a positive
difference in a kid's life. . . .
Working together to achieve your goals—
a winning game and a winning life.

—BOB STALEY, CLASS OF 1970

Vocation takes many forms. Retired classmate Bob
Staley has found his vocation in coaching youth
sports. He sees sports as promoting the well-being of
mind, body, and spirit. Bob notes that "the one thing
I tell my teams at the beginning of the season is that
no matter what happens, win or lose, they are all win-
ners because they are doing something positive with
their lives." While Bob wouldn't describe himself as

religious in the traditional way, his coaching has a spiritual character, as it promotes values, teamwork, and mutual support. Sports teams can be catalysts of creating what Martin Luther King Jr., referred to as the "Beloved Community."

Who might you be called to mentor? How might you enable a younger or less experienced person to learn the fundamentals of a creative, athletic, or artistic endeavor, and see their proficiency as part of their spiritual and relational growth?

Embodied Spirit, I give thanks for the wondrous integration of body, mind, and spirit.
Help me to use my gifts to inspire new generations in the art of living.

12.

Often when you think you're at
the end of something,
You're at the beginning of something else.

—FRED ROGERS

In the circle of life, every ending can give birth to
a new beginning. Every beginning requires us to
jettison parts of our past. The space in between can
be seen as both a wilderness and a womb. Wild beasts
will be there and moments of confusion. There will
also be the birth of a new self with expanded interests
and abilities. The space in between can be frightening,
and we may need spiritual midwives to help us in the

birthing process. Still, the great "what's next?" can be the time of our lives.

What gift do you have for the next stage of life? What might you need to give up for new birth to occur?

God of new beginnings, may your Spirit of Adventure be born in me. May I be patient with the unsettled and unknown.

13.

Living each day as if it were your last . . .
means to live fully, authentically
and spontaneously
with nothing being held back.

—JACK CANFIELD

This is the time of our lives. Now is the only moment we have. One of the parents of the faith, the early-Christian spiritual teacher Iranaeus, asserted that the glory of God is a fully alive person. Experiencing ourselves as fully alive comes and goes, of course, but we know those moments when we are completely in the moment, feeling Life flow through us, experiencing the ecstasy of simply

breathing. We don't have to do anything remarkable to be fully alive. Right here is heaven. This moment holds enlightenment. Behold, this is a day of new beginnings, a day of wonder and beauty, love and challenge, healing and transforming.

When have you felt fully alive? What burdens do you need to release to delight in the Holy Here-and-Now?

Holy Breath, let me see everlasting life as I play with a grandchild, tutor at school, write a poem, protest injustice, gaze at a sunset, or pick litter up at a park. Let every moment be enlightening and transforming.

14.

In retirement, I have taken up
watercolors once again.
I bring a blank piece of paper to life
with each stroke of my brush. . . .
When I paint, I share a part of me.

—ESTHER ALFEREZ HOGAN, CLASS OF 1970

We are all artists of our experience. Each moment has the potential for creativity. My classmate Esther Alferez delights in the visual arts. Always creative, she has reclaimed the artist within during her retirement, and now her art adds to the beauty of the universe. My artistry is with words and images;

this book is my creative synthesis of the twenty-six letters of the alphabet, the wisdom of sages, and the contours of the English language. While there are many avenues along the "artist's way," when we create, using the unique materials and gifts of our lives, we become companions with the Artist of the Universe, who brings forth galaxies and planets, flora and fauna, right whales and soaring eagles, guided by the Divine vision of truth, beauty, and goodness.

Where are you called to be an artist? What materials of your life—experiences, gifts, talents, environment—can be the media of your own artistry? What beauty can you share with the universe?

Artist of the Universe, inspire me to be Your companion artist, bringing forth beauty for the world around me.

15.

One of the secrets to a happy life
is continuous small treats.

—IRIS MURDOCH

In retirement, we may discover that we don't have to put off having fun. As the saying goes, "It's never too late to have a happy childhood." Treats come in all kinds, and they don't need to be deferred till tomorrow. When I think of my "treats," what comes to mind is a walk on the beach or in the woods, the strong cup of coffee I am enjoying right now, sitting in the garden basking in the sun, watching a British murder mystery, reading a novel in the middle of the day, listening

to a song from my youth or a symphony as a study break, making a burrito, taking a walk with a friend, reading the Hardy Boys mysteries with my grandchildren, phone conversations with friends far away, or just pausing to sit with my wife Kate after a morning's study or writing. Writing this text is a treat. It is a joy to begin each morning with meditation, a cup of coffee, writing for the pure joy of it, and then going to the beach or the woods for a walk.

What treats spice up *your* day? What treats, deferred because of your work, can you enjoy in retirement? I believe God offers each one of us daily delights!

Help me rejoice, Spirit of Joy, in small things that give shape to a good life.

16.

You don't stop laughing when you grow old,
you grow old when you stop laughing.

—ANONYMOUS

"Angels can fly because they can take themselves lightly," wrote the philosopher G. K. Chesterton. The same principle applies to retirees: if we can stop taking ourselves so seriously, we may find ourselves soaring, spiritually and emotionally. At our age, we will have unexpected surprises and mishaps. We may play a mean game of tennis or pickleball— and then end up limping for three days. We may get all sorts of nicknames from our grandchildren and

younger relatives. We may have to chuckle ironically when despite our attempts to be cool, someone calls us "elderly." Laughter has been called the best medicine, an adage that scientific research has confirmed.

So rejoice, have fun, laugh at your foibles, don't worry about making a mistake. Your laughter may be the tonic you need today.

Loving God, help me take myself lightly, so that my laughter might join the angels' chorus.

17.

Habit has a kind of poetry.

—SIMONE DE BEAUVOIR

A good life involves the right blend of order and chaos, predictability and spontaneity, familiarity and novelty—and a healthy retirement involves habits held flexibly. A certain order along with openness to surprise characterizes the contours of a well-spent day. Summer and winter, seedtime and harvest, equinox and solstice: creative habits can bring the joy of the familiar in an ever-changing world.

What are your most joyful habits? What rituals give poetry to your day? What new practices might deepen your spirituality or add zest to life?

Faithful Spirit, thank You for the interplay of ritual and novelty. Great is Your faithfulness, for Your mercies are new every morning.

18.

Retirement doesn't have to mean
giving up what I enjoy!
I still consult, as needed, because I like working
in the school districts who ask for my help.
But now I work on my own terms.

—DEBRA CHEW QUAN, CLASS OF 1970

For those of us who found meaning and enjoyment in our professions, retirement may involve maintaining our professional lives—but on our own terms. While we can chart entirely new courses, delighting in new talents, we may also discover that what gave our lives meaning professionally is still meaningful. Freed

from the old constraints, our work becomes a grace and blessing, a chance to help others and share our wisdom.

What talents from your professional life do you still want to share? Where might you share these talents? How might these gifts evolve as you grow older?

Creative Spirit, reveal to me new possibilities. Show me ways to share my skills to bring joy to others, as well as meaning to my life.

19.

Don't simply retire from something;
have something to retire to.

—HARRY EMERSON FOSDICK

In retirement, we don't need an agenda, a list of things to check off each day, or a bucket list of things to accomplish; life throws us curves, and we may find ourselves on pathways we never imagined. Still, we need a horizon of possibility to give our lives meaning and hope. As we look for the moral and spiritual arcs flowing through our lives, we can use them to orientate ourselves toward wholeness and creativity in the context of the world's needs.

What vision wakes you up in the morning? What adventure lures you forward? What are you retiring *to*—or what is the next step of your retirement adventure? With a vision, you can move forward with hope and agency through the storms of aging.

Guide my steps, loving Spirit. May each day give birth to new adventures as I pilgrim day by day.

20.

Few societies have come to grips
with the new demography. . . .
More than half of the very old
now live without a spouse
and we have fewer children than ever before,
yet we give virtually no thought
to how we will live out our later years alone.

—ATUL GAWANDE

The changing demographics of aging challenge us to envision our future in new ways. While a joyful retirement is not just about our financial security, our financial resources matter. We need to use our

financial assets wisely, just as we must also take care of our physical well-being through a healthy lifestyle and our intellectual, emotional, and spiritual well-being through cultivating creative endeavors, relationships, and deeper prayer lives. While we cannot guarantee the future, we must mindfully imagine the next twenty-five years' amazing adventures as well as financial challenges.

Do you have a financial plan for the years ahead? It is never too late to plan for a joyful retirement.

Help me, fellow Pilgrim, to use my time, talent, and treasure creatively, wisely, and compassionately.

21.

I am no longer accepting the
things I cannot change.
I am changing the things I cannot accept.

—ATTRIBUTED TO ANGELA DAVIS

The Serenity Prayer counsels us to accept the things we cannot change. Certain situations and events are beyond our control, and we need to learn to adapt to these inevitabilities; as author Judith Viorst noted, the aging process is filled with "necessary losses" in terms of physical diminishment, grief, and professional status. Still, acceptance does not mean passivity. We can become agents of our own destiny, seeking to be

as creative as possible despite life's limitations. Nor should we be apathetic in a world filled with injustice. No longer fearful of professional repercussions, we can pray and protest, agitate and advocate, condemn and challenge . . . and even be willing to go to jail to protest injustice. Let us change what is in our power, and protest what we cannot accept. Our grandchildren, and children everywhere, depend on us.

What aspects of our society can you no longer accept? What things in life do you need to accept with grace?

God of compassion and confrontation, give me courage to both accept life's inevitable losses and confront injustice in the world around me.

22.

I have always noticed that
deeply and truly religious
persons are fond of a joke,
and I am suspicious of those who aren't.

—ALFRED NORTH WHITEHEAD

This statement by one of the twentieth century's greatest philosophers captures the spirit of a joyful retirement—the ability to have fun and enjoy moments of delight. Laughter, as *Reader's Digest* noted, is the best medicine. Age is sometimes filled with aches and pains, but if we can learn to laugh at ourselves, we'll find it is also filled with humorous moments. Laugh-

ing lifts our spirits, connects us with other people, and enables us to accept our fallibility and move forward with hope.

What makes you laugh? When did you last roar with laughter? What activity might you do just for the fun of it?

Thank you, Laughing God, for moments of hilarity and delight. Help me to smile and laugh and bring joy wherever I go.

23.

Retire from your job
but never from meaningful projects.

—STEPHEN COVEY

Retirement may involve greater leisure. It may involve withdrawal from the activities that defined your work life. But a joyful retirement is grounded in both doing and being, action and rest, and involvement and withdrawal. Our gifts are meant to grow and not atrophy in retirement. Our projects can be artistic, relational, scholarly, political, or spiritual. There are many ways to live a joyful retirement, especially when we find creative ways to nurture ourselves and those around us.

What gets you up in the morning? What projects delight you and give you a sense of meaning? How might you serve those around you with your unique gifts?

Let the energy of love flow through me, Spirit of Joy, filling me with imagination and delight and willingness to share my gifts with the world.

24.

Riding is great. Riding for a
cause is even greater.
I am on an epic ride for truth and redemption.

—HY LIBBY, CLASS OF 1970

My classmate Hy Libby motorcycles for a cause
in retirement. He is committed to supporting
veterans, most especially Vietnam veterans. Hy has
found that small gifts, inspired by love and respect,
can change lives. We can share in the healing process
simply by listening to a Vietnam vet tell their story,
reaching out to a person of another faith or ethnic
background, standing beside a marginalized person

when they are subject to racist taunts, or giving our time coaching, mentoring, or tutoring.

What volunteer activities do you feel called to undertake? How might you be useful to forgotten members of your community?

Open my senses, Spirit, to the intersection of my gifts and the world's needs. Let me share my love with the forgotten and marginalized.

25.

Life was meant to be lived, and curiosity must be kept alive.

—ELEANOR ROOSEVELT

We live in an amazing universe, and we are amazing ourselves. The journey of self-discovery is infinite—and we are also connected with an intricate and interdependent planet, whose wonders would take more than a lifetime to fathom. Just think of all the amazing things that have emerged in our lifetime—computers, cell phones, internet and social media, Moon and Mars landings, organ transplants, genetic technology, immediate breaking news, heart bypasses

and hip replacements, and our expanding knowledge of land, air, and sea life.

What things pique your curiosity? What new things would you like to learn? What faraway places would you like to explore? What aspects of your own inner space inspire curiosity and gratitude? Retirement is a time for exploration. Freed from the obligations of employment, we can, with Buzz Lightyear from *Toy Story*, go forth toward "infinity and beyond." So stay curious! Stay alive! Look ahead for the great "what's next?"

Adventurous Spirit, thank You for infinite horizons.

26.

But unless we are creators, we
are not fully alive. . . .
Creativity is a way of living life,
no matter our vocation or how
we earn our living.

—MADELEINE L'ENGLE

Creativity takes many forms, from woodworking to writing, bird-watching to gardening, telling bedtime stories to coaching sports. The point is to bring something new into the world. The goal is to share our gifts with others, and in the sharing, expand your own

gifts. In fact, each moment of experience is a creative act, bringing together a plethora of experiences along with our own feelings and responses. We are always creating, and we can become intentional creators.

How might you enhance your creative potential? Make your life a work of art—whether protesting injustice, working at the polls, or planting a garden. Bring something beautiful to the world.

Creative Spirit, let Your creativity inspire my own.

27.

We need to make room for younger people,
new ideas and new ways of doing things.
The cycle of life needs to continue.

—DEBRA CHEW QUAN, CLASS OF 1970

Classmate Debra Chew Quan sees retirement as a necessary contribution to the creativity of others. Younger generations need us to make space for their creativity and fresh visions. The experiences of youth bring new ideas and new approaches to problem-solving. Elders like myself can learn from teen environmentalist Greta Thunberg and gun-safety activists from Parkland High. While it is right and good for us to remain professionally involved and passionate about

vocations and causes to which we've devoted our lives, now is the time to become mentors and cheerleaders rather than high control decision-makers.

Where do you need to let go so that younger generations gain experience and expertise? What are the biggest challenges you face when stepping aside to make room for fresh perspectives?

As new generations are emerging, with new visions and dreams, help me, Spirit, to be patient and affirmative, making way for new possibilities.

28.

Whoever said anybody has a right to give up?

—MARIAN WRIGHT EDELMAN

Stepping aside does not mean passivity, nor does it mean giving up on the causes and vocations around which we shaped our lives. No longer tethered to regular office hours or narrow institutional accountability, we can follow our political and spiritual passions. We can become the protester, advocate, hands-on volunteer, and activist that we tamped down when we had other responsibilities. We can take chances. We may choose to use our gifts and experience to transform the institutions to which we devoted a lifetime

of employment. Or we may simply pray, if we can no longer protest, recognizing that ten million retirees at prayer may be catalytic in God's realm coming to be on earth as it is in heaven. New possibilities and energies emerge when we discover we still can make a difference and that God needs us to respond to the evils and injustices of our time.

How might you awaken new passions to propel you on the journey of personal and social transformation?

Spirit of Justice, help me shape Your vision in response to the world's needs.

29.

The more sand has escaped from
the hourglass of our life,
the clearer we should see through it.

—JOHANN PAUL FRIEDRICH RICHTER

Now that I am nearly sixty-nine, I am aware of the brevity of life. When I hear of a celebrity, colleague, or politician dying, I count the years between my age and theirs. I wonder if this is the time I too have left. This may sound morbid, but this attitude can also be a reminder to make each day count: To seize the day! To seize the moment! To treat this moment as if it is the only one I have, unique, irreplaceable,

and wonderful. To see the ordinary as spiritual and the spiritual as ordinary. To see this day in all its ordinariness as the sanctuary of time, and to live as fully as possible.

What do you need to embrace in this moment of time? How can you best imagine the future and still live in the now? This is the day that God has made, that Life has given you—rejoice and be glad in it.

Spirit of time and space, eternity and temporality, let me rejoice in this moment. Let this now be everlasting and eternal.

30.

We have to be braver than we think we can be,
because God is constantly calling us
to be more than we are.

—MADELEINE L'ENGLE

Retirement is not for the faint-hearted. It is an adventure, and like all adventures, it involves risk and opportunity. It takes courage to let go of our professional personas, our status in the community, our familiar spots, and venture forth to a new land, without the "essentials" of our previous lives. Yet this is what the call of God is about: inviting us to new dimensions of life, to imagine fresh horizons, to cre-

ate and re-create the selves we are becoming. God calls us to be more than we can ask or imagine. And when God calls, God promises, "I will be with you. I will guide your path. I will present possibilities in the form of events, persons, and opportunities, and then leave it to you to embrace or reject. Know that in success or failure, embrace or denial, I am with you, and My loving light will be enough for the next step of your journey."

Where are you challenged to summon extra courage? What horizons are both frightening and exciting?

Show me the path ahead, Spirit, one step at a time.

31.

In retirement, I can create a completely new life
and do all the things I've thought about
but didn't have time to do until now.

—ALAN OKAGAKI, CLASS OF 1970

After a successful career in nonprofit organizations, classmate Alan Okagaki practices what he
preaches. He recently enrolled in a PhD program in
political philosophy, now that he has the time to pursue one of the roads not traveled in his professional
life. We are not bound to repeat the past in retirement.
Nor are we required to stay the course and pursue the
interests and skills that characterized our professional

lives. Behold, as scripture says, we can do "a new thing." We can make a U-turn that may even surprise us. There are many selves and many paths for each of us. Many of our gifts are like buried treasure, currently unknown even to us. The joy is in the exploration, and the discovery of new adventures, new gifts, and new ways to bring joy to the world.

What are your roads not taken? What parts of yourself, so far unexplored, lure you forward? How might you explore these new paths?

**Let me explore the wonders of my life, Spirit.
Let me welcome change and imperfection
as I take new paths of self-discovery.**

32.

What is the great thing for which
you would sacrifice your life?
. . . What is the call of life to
you—do you know it?

—JOSEPH CAMPBELL

E ach of us, regardless of what others see in us or
how they evaluate our impact on the world, have
a "great work" that calls us forward. Your great work
may be learning to swim and pursue public speaking at
seventy. It may be standing with the marginalized and
oppressed and lifting your voice in protest. It may be
internalizing the pain others feel through poverty and

homelessness and making a commitment in retirement to overseas volunteer work, inner-city mentoring, or challenging injustice and dishonesty in the political realm. These paths will all require sacrifice—and possibly risk—but our souls expand, and our hearts find fulfillment in the journey, even if it first appears as an impossible dream.

What heroic journey calls you forward? What are the risks and possibilities in the adventures ahead?

Awaken me, Spirit of Adventure, to the amazing journey that awaits me. Challenge me to explore new possibilities.

33.

Age is a question of mind over matter.
If you don't mind, it doesn't matter.

—SATCHEL PAIGE

Baseball Hall of Fame pitcher Satchel Paige, whose baseball career spanned five decades, knew that age was a matter of attitude as well as years. As long as we have a vision, we are young. Our spirits soar, inspiring creativity in mind, body, spirit, vocation, and relationships. A youthful spirit challenges limitations as we explore our dreams. We might discover a motorcyclist or a marathon runner within us. We might unearth a poet or a novelist. We might have an

inner scientist, gardener, global traveler, or healer. If the Infinite—the Holy—is present in finite creatures like us, then each of us is the child of infinity. Each of us shares in eternity, and the energy of the Big Bang and Divine possibility dwell in us.

What are your self-imposed limits? As you face them, remember the words of Ephesians 3:20: God's power at work within you is able "to accomplish abundantly far more than all we can ask or imagine"—and then go forth on a holy adventure with God as your companion and guide.

Open my mind, Spirit, to wonder and possibility. Tear down the walls of limitation that I might explore new possibilities.

34.

These days, if you retire at 66, you may have
twenty or thirty years left, or even more.
Don't waste it listening to the voices
in your head from the past!

—JOHN PERRY

Philosopher and blogger John Perry reminds us that retirement is a time for new adventures. We don't need to be hemmed in by yesterday's constraints or achievements. Retirement can be an opportunity for experimentation, exploring the roads not (yet) taken. We can forge new identities without worry about success or failure. In the process, we may have to discard

some voices from our past—the voices of perfectionism, people-pleasing, judgment, limitation. When God told the prophet Isaiah, "Behold, I do a new thing," the Divine Spirit was revealing the power of the future.

What past voices and expectations limit you? What new roads draw you forward?

Spirit of Possibility, free me from the voices of limitation so that I can be faithful to Your dream for my life.

35.

Now I know only in part;
then I will know fully.

—1 CORINTHIANS 13:12

We know in part. Our awareness of ourselves, God, and the future is limited. This is both humbling and inviting. On the one hand, we don't know what risks and crises lie ahead. We cannot calculate in advance our own or our partner's health, or the progress of our investments. On the other hand, we cannot predict what positive adventures will come our way. Our future is open, and that is exciting as well as challenging. False starts and dead ends, even fail-

ures, in our retirement journey are not the end of the world. They may, in fact, lead to new adventures. Not knowing the hour of our death, or how long we have, invites us to take each day as holy and unrepeatable. We are in process, we are growing, and the adventure continues.

Looking at your life thus far, where have unexpected adventures emerged? During this stage of your life, how can you make the most of each day and not let opportunities pass?

God of time and space, awaken in me a spirit of adventure. Show me new possibilities, and give me the courage to explore them.

36.

Oh my friend, why do you . . .
care so much about
laying up the greatest amount of
money and honor and reputation,
and so little about wisdom and truth
and the greatest improvement of the soul. . . ?

—SOCRATES

Socrates reminds us to cultivate our spiritual lives.
Property and fame will not last, but love and wisdom are our companions in all life's changes. Let us
cast our eyes on eternity while treasuring time. Most
of us will not be called to literally abandon everything

and become hermits devoted to prayer—but all of us can let go of our dependency on possessions and status to focus primarily on God.

What is most important to you in your life? What is your ultimate concern, the value or values around which you live your life and make your decisions? What will you prioritize now that you are retired? What do you need to prune away to live more abundantly and discern your vocation during retirement?

Give me the insight, Wise Spirit, to discern the important and the unimportant, and let go of everything that stands between me and fulfilling Your dream for my life.

37.

Know your financial status and finances.
You need to know your resources
and what you need to live well.

—DEBRA CHEW QUAN, CLASS OF 1970

While money and fame are not the ultimate values in a good life, living gracefully in retirement involves mindful financial planning. Having enough financial resources reduces stress, enables us to devote more time to self-improvement, and gives us the ability to contribute to causes that are important to us. Our finances are sacred tools that provide learning and travel opportunities, as well as support for our

grandchildren in their education, a hospitable home for friends and family to visit, and largesse to organizations that reflect our values.

As you take an inventory of your financial situation, how would you describe it? Will you need to take on part-time employment to subsidize your retirement funds? If so, what would you like to do? How would you like your finances to reflect your values? Care for your finances as you do for your physical and spiritual health and relationships. Let your values guide your finances, so that they will be a blessing to you and the larger community.

God of all creation, may I use my financial resources wisely and may they bring joy to me, my loved ones, and the larger world.

38.

Do you want a vision for the last third of your life
that will give you a reason to
get up in the morning
and be excited for the day ahead? . . .
Do you want direction and purpose in your life
even when you become sick, lose loved ones,
or encounter many of the other changes
that aging is likely to bring?

—HAROLD KOENIG

All of us need a polestar. A vision of possibility. A far horizon toward which we are drawn to provide energy for today's challenges. Having a vision of the

future, a sense of meaning, roots each encounter and each day in a larger story. Each day builds on yesterday and leans toward tomorrow as our lives become a holy adventure. When tragedy happens, it may turn our lives upside down; we may grieve and feel alone— but if we have a polestar, we will find meaning even in challenging times. The spiritual end goals toward which we sojourn will keep us afloat and draw us forward through the dark valley that often precedes the emergence of God's healing light.

What gets you up in the morning? What far horizon draws you forward?

Thank you, God of Adventure, for passion and possibility.

39.

The only way to avoid being miserable
is not to have enough leisure to wonder
whether you are happy or not.

—GEORGE BERNARD SHAW

Don't rust out in retirement. Stay awake, stay alive, and stay busy with creative and meaningful activity. Boredom deadens the spirit, and apathy undermines physical and spiritual well-being. During retirement, we need to find the golden mean between sabbath rest and meaningful activity. We need time for contemplation and self-examination—and we also need to create and congregate, to make new friends and explore uncharted territories.

How would you evaluate your balance of rest and activity? Do you feel bored or overburdened? What might help you find the right level of creative activity?

Help me, Spirit, to find a dynamic balance of rest and activity that my life might be meaningful and lively.

40.

Not all who wander are lost.

—J. R. R. TOLKIEN

While the accepted wisdom of some retirement advisors is that you need a plan, with clear goals and objectives, to enjoy a happy retirement, I believe it is equally important to make room for meandering and synchronicity. If we see retirement as a time for experimentation, then we must assume all sorts of unexpected adventures. We may also anticipate times of wilderness meandering, surveying the scenario of your new life without agenda or purpose. We need not be purpose-driven in retirement, especially if that was

our previous modus operandi. There are times when we need to simply let things happen, throw away our calendar and agenda, and open ourselves to what life gives us. There is grace in not-doing.

Do you allow time for graceful spontaneity and unexpected adventures? Your path in retirement may at times require going with the flow and letting the stream of life carry you around new bends to unanticipated vistas.

God of surprising love, help me let go of control and immerse myself in the graceful streams of life that flow from the river of Your love.

41.

There are two periods in our lives
when we have exceptional freedom:
at college-age and when we begin
our retirement years.

—JIMMY CARTER

College can be a time and place for wandering and experimentation, taking a variety of personal paths with little risk, and within the experimentation, we may find our vocation. The same applies to retirement. We can experiment. Try new things. Even walk a bit on the wild side! Explore new ways of being ourselves and new vocational adventures. Sure, we have

obligations—marriage and grandparenting, perhaps, and our volunteer and institutional commitments— but beyond that, the only limits are those of health, finances, location, and our own imagination. Many of these limits can be challenged by changes in lifestyle, a change of address, and the willingness to let your sense of self expand as you look toward new horizons of self-discovery.

If you could do anything, what would it be? What part of your self lies undiscovered? What vocational vision has been hovering for decades, waiting for your embrace?

Loving and adventurous Spirit, let my newfound freedom bring joy to myself and the world.

42.

We grow spiritually much
more by doing it wrong
than by doing it right.

—RICHARD ROHR

Retirement beckons us to see our lives as a won-drous experiment. To see ourselves in the spirit of a scientific adventure in which failures and mistakes are stepping-stones on the way to discovery. Retirement is not an invitation to license or harmful behaviors, of course, but when we faithfully recognize our fallibility, take a few spiritual chances and succeed and fail in new relationships and projects, we are

simply awakening new paths of self-awareness. Each choice leads to others, but no choice is final. Even dead ends can lead to alternative pathways. Grace abounds. God is always presenting us with possibilities, even after mistakes. Our mistakes may be the open doors to unexpected encounters and greater understanding of ourselves and others.

What risks might you be willing to take to gain new insights, experiences, or spiritual growth?

God of all pathways, remind me that even my mistakes can open the door to new and positive possibilities.

43.

Simple things are what life is made of.

—DEBBIE JONES HALLYBURTON, CLASS OF 1970

"It's a gift to be simple," so goes the Shaker classic. In a similar vein, the Danish philosopher Soren Kierkegaard asserted that "purity of heart is to do one thing." Simplicity of spirit reminds us that our lives unfold one moment at a time . . . and the world is saved one moment, encounter, and day at a time. A good life in retirement involves moving and stretching, calling friends, getting together for lunch, watching the sun rise and set, spending quiet moments in contemplation, and for some of us, reexperiencing our own childhoods

as we play with grandchildren. Each moment can be holy. Each encounter can be a blessing, each breath a prayer. It truly is a gift to be simple. Each moment, where we are right *now*, is the valley of delight.

What simple gifts renew your spirit? What daily practices give shape to your life?

God of small and large adventures, open my senses and spirit to the joy of simplicity.

44.

Be patient with one another.

—COLOSSIANS 3:13

Retirement—and the aging process as a whole—requires patience. We may not move as quickly as we once did. We experience aches and pains attendant to the aging process. Sometimes we may find it difficult to remember the right word. Some of this can be remedied through medication and exercise, but the answers lie as much in acceptance as agency, patience as practical responses. At the same time, we need to be patient with others as well, looking beyond our self-interest to experience the needs of others. Others

are also experiencing the challenges of retirement and aging. Patience enables us to see ourselves and others with greater compassion and discover the wonder of those around us in their unique and tragic beauty.

In what ways are you impatient with yourself? In what ways do others try your patience? How might you be more accepting and compassionate toward your own—and others'—humanity?

Let me find contentment and joy in this moment, Spirit, changing what I cannot accept, accepting what I cannot change, and having compassion toward everyone I meet.

45.

And Abraham and Sarah
journeyed forth by stages.

—GENESIS 12:8

In the wilderness trek to their promised land, Sarah and Abraham learn to be patient. They plant altars wherever they stop to remind them that God is with them and that wherever they are, they can find meaning and purpose. In a similar way, joyful retirement involves both predictable and surprising stages. Like Abraham and Sarah, we need to erect altars for the journey—prayer, meditation, visioning, rest, contemplation, and mission—to enable each stage to be part

of a holy adventure. With a sense of Divine companionship, each stage is an opportunity to deepen our spiritual life and grow in relationship to God and our loved ones.

What stage do you see yourself in the retirement process? What stages of retirement do you perceive as most challenging?

God of the pilgrimage, let me see You in each stage retirement brings. Remind me to erect altars of prayerful self-awareness and gratitude at every stage.

46.

Let there be spaces in your togetherness.

—KAHLIL GIBRAN

Retirement creates new contours for our relationships. Many couples who are both retired will initially spend more time together than at any time in their relationship. My wife and I enjoy each other's company, but we have had to establish new routines to balance my wife's activist extroversion and my scholarly introversion. We've discovered we have different needs for solitude, companionship, work, and play, and we have had to be intentional about finding spaces in our togetherness. Life is a yin-yang of solitude and

relationship, of finding the happy medium that suits each partner. Partners committed to a joyful retirement need to give and take, to adapt, to loosen their grip on their individual agendas. In doing so, they may experience a new togetherness and greater joy in their relationships.

How much solitude do you need? How much solitude and relatedness does your partner need? In what ways can you find a happy medium?

Loving God, help me respond to my partner's needs, even as I nurture my own.

47.

But know it's never fifty-fifty in a marriage.
It's always seventy-thirty, or sixty-forty.

—JODI PICOULT

The contours of relationships are constantly alter-
ing. For one season, you might be making most of
the effort, joining work, parenting, and housekeeping.
Then life shifts, and you are in a recess period, experiencing the gifts of time and freedom. As yet another
season comes, you find yourself in the caregiver role
for your parents or spouse. Later, someone else cares
for you in your infirmity. Healthy relationships are
like the ebb and flow of the sea; everything is in flux,

and change is the only constant. We need to embrace both agency and receptivity with grace and gratitude.

What is the current balance of give-and-take in your relationship or relationships? Are you a giver or receiver? Which role is most challenging for you? What spiritual practices enable you to live with the ebb and flow of relationships?

Give me the grace, Companion Spirit,
to give and receive, to care for my loved ones
with compassion and accept their loving care
with gratitude.

48.

For better, for worse, for richer, for poorer,
in sickness and in health, to love and to cherish
as long as we both shall live.

—TRADITIONAL MARRIAGE VOWS

Since no one knows what the future will bring, we need to make a commitment to be faithful in any imaginable—and sometimes unimaginable—future. Retirement is hopefully full of recreation, travel, shared times with friends and family, and common values expressed in our spiritual and political lives. It may also involve illness and decline, physically and cognitively. Each one of us is just a footstep—or a

fall—away from disability, and we need people who are committed to us regardless of what the future brings. Faithful retirement is about caring for each other, bearing each other's burdens, and sharing each other's joys. There is beauty in devoted love—even when it is embodied at the memory-care center or hospital.

How might you prepare spiritually to care for your life companion in difficult times?

Spirit of Love, give me courage, patience, persistence, and love in all the seasons of our relationship.

49.

I volunteer at an animal shelter
three times each week
taking care of animals that people have cast off.
I have a sense of pride that I have
made a difference. . . .

—DEBBIE HAY SANTOS, CLASS OF 1970

We save the world one act at a time. No act of kindness is too small in the healing of the world. When my classmate Debbie Hay Santos brings love to the animal shelter, she is living out Jesus' counsel, "as you did to the least of these, you have done unto me." While Debbie may not think of caring for animals in

spiritual terms, I believe that whenever we contribute to the well-being of a fellow creature, we are playing our part in making the world a better place. We are healing the world. As the companion of a ninety-pound Golden Doodle, I know how the slightest kindness is immediately registered with joyful tail wagging or a happy bark. The love we share with our companion animals radiates across the neighborhood and planet and tips the scale toward healing and beauty in our often chaotic and uncivil world.

How might you contribute to the well-being of the non-human world, whether personally or politically?

Spirit of Life, attune me to the cries of the non-human as well as human worlds.

50.

Grandparents sort of sprinkle stardust over the lives of little children.

—ALEX HALEY

No longer tied to the constraints of parenting, grandparents can push the spiritual, emotional, and relational envelopes. No longer attached to specific results, often unbothered by breaking society's "rules," they can be purveyors of joy and hilarity. They can be love-finders and fun-fomenters, the guardians of imagination and the champions of adventure.

How has grandparenting opened your life to new vistas of experience? If you aren't a grandparent or your grandchildren are grown, what children might you appropriately "adopt"? It is never too late to have a happy childhood along with your grandchildren. Life is magical. Stardust is real. Each home has a wardrobe leading to Narnia, and you can catch the train to Hogwarts from your own backyard. Every day is a holy adventure.

Spirit of magic and adventure, may I be a love-finder and a giver of stardust to the children in my life.

51.

By the standards of the European
industrial world
we are poor peasants, but when
I embrace my grandfather
I experience a sense of richness
as though I am a note
in the heartbeats of the very universe.

—TAYEB SALIH

After decades in the workplace, as grandparents we
need to learn a different kind of excellence—the
excellence of caring companionship, unrestrained

imagination, unambiguous support, and unfettered acceptance. Young children don't need our money as much as they need our love and imagination. They need our presence as companions in their journeys of adventure, companions who consistently radiate radical and unconditional love and acceptance. Let us bring eternity to each moment of our children's lives, whether they are biological grandchildren, children we tutor and mentor, or children for whom we advocate. Let us be good ancestors, building the future of our children one loving act at a time.

What richness can you share with future generations? What gift of joy can you present the children in your life?

As I enter this stage of my life, Spirit, help me radiate love, imagination, and care for the future.

52.

Reading should not be presented to
children as a chore or duty.
It should be offered to them as a precious gift.

—KATE DICAMILLO

Reading has been central to my relationship with my son as well as my grandchildren. Over the years, we read nearly every morning, books ranging from *Good Night, Good Night, Construction Site* to the Hardy Boys and Steinbeck's *Travels with Charley* and now *Watership Down*. Reading stimulates the imagination and opens lifelong doors of wonder and learning. It also offers topics of conversation and opportunities

to hear children's ideas and questions. We need to listen before we lecture; we need to be willing to learn as much as we teach. Together, adults and children can help each other explore what it means to be a compassionate and caring, a strong and persistent human in our complex world.

What books shaped your life as a child? Have you shared them with the children in your life? How might you use books to open yourself to the curiosity and wonder of childhood?

Amid, the busyness of life, Spirit, remind me to read, to listen, and to respond with love and companionship.

53.

I am looking forward to our reunion,
to reunite with people with whom
I have a shared history.

—ERNIE DE LOS SANTOS, CLASS OF 1970

Our fiftieth high school reunion was canceled due to the pandemic—but the canceled reunion inspired me to reach out to classmates, to sponsor a Zoom conversation, and then to include some of my classmates' reflections in this text. Reclaiming meaningful relationships sheds light on the past and gives hope for the future. Shared histories bind us in a common journey. Stories and experiences make us what we are

today, and in embracing our pasts, we can chart new pathways to the future, guided in part by lessons we learned in our youth. How good it is to reclaim friend-ships as catalysts for gratitude for yesterday and hope for tomorrow.

Do you still have relationships with high school classmates? What persons from high school or college would you love to encounter today? How might you accomplish this?

God of past, present, and future, thank You for the gifts of the past. May they be catalysts for new adventures, inspiring me to hope and action.

54.

Whatever is true, whatever is
honorable, whatever is just,
whatever is pure, whatever is pleasing,
whatever is commendable,
if there is any excellence and if there
is anything worthy of praise,
think about these things.

—PHILIPPIANS 4:8

Retirement and the aging process can bring negative stereotypes to the surface, many of which we may internalize. We wonder if the best years are

behind us. We fixate on aches and pains. We worry we will be marginalized and viewed as nuisances. We wish we looked younger. But there is another spiritual path. Without denying the necessary losses that accompany aging and retirement, we can accentuate the positive gains: wisdom, perspective, life experience, inner beauty, faithful relationships, resilience.

What negative images of retirement and aging surface in your consciousness? How can you prune negative thinking so you can see life as it is in all its wondrous complexity, intricate ambiguity, and tragic beauty?

Enable me, Spirit of Love, to place negativity in perspective, accent the positive, and claim my agency in healing the world.

55.

For old people beauty doesn't come
free with the hormones,
the way it does for the young...
It has to do with who the person is.

—URSULA LE GUIN

Often in retirement, we feel as if beauty has left us behind. We think no one will give us a second look; we're just another old person. Still, there is a deeper beauty than skin, age, and figure: the beauty of character, wisdom, and integrity. The beauty of compassion and sacrifice. The beauty that shines through our wrinkles and waistlines. Indeed, we have earned

our wrinkles by decades of learning from experience and the willingness now to share our wisdom when it is needed. As we age, we may discover that we have become elders, sages, wise ones, crones, and wizards—and with these new identities comes the beauty of wholeness, love, and commitment to be a "good ancestor" for generations beyond our time.

Do you ever feel left behind in the world of productivity, power, and youth? Looking more deeply, what wisdom shines through your wrinkles? What beauty fills your spirit? How can you share both with those around you?

Beautiful God, help me to claim the beauty of aging.

56.

For surely I know the plans I have for you,
says the Lord, plans for your
welfare and not for harm,
to give you a future with hope.

—JEREMIAH 29:11

Retirement can be challenging. We may have left
our employment and moved to a new home. We
still may grieve the losses involved in retirement—
structure, professional prestige and respect, financial
largesse. All this means that familiar landmarks may
have disappeared. Even if we have prepared well, we
may worry about becoming irrelevant, a nuisance

rather than a resource. At such times, we need to remember that our lives are part of a larger story—God's story. God has plans for us for a future and a hope. And God's vision is waiting for our response: our willingness to move forward, taking responsibility for our lives, becoming agents of our destiny, in companionship with the God of yesterday, today, and tomorrow.

As you look at your life today, what positive visions of the future are emerging for you, inviting you to joyful agency and creativity?

Artist of the Universe, help me to trust Your vision when mine is uncertain.

57.

So we do not lose heart.
Even though our outer nature is wasting away,
our inner nature is being renewed day by day.

—2 CORINTHIANS 4:16

Retirement is often when we awaken to the challenges of the aging process. In addition to plans for hobbies and excursions, these years may bring knee and hip replacements, diminished physical strength, and changes in our sex lives. With retirement, also comes a greater sense of our mortality. And yet, despite the physical challenges of aging, retirement can be a

time for inner exploration, providing new opportunities to deepen our spiritual and intellectual lives.

Where are you experiencing physical diminishment? How are you responding to physical changes? What deepens your spirit? There is a deeper reality that transcends aging—God's infinite love coursing through our cells and souls, inviting us to become pilgrims on a never-ending adventure. What practices awaken you to God's energy of love flowing through you?

God of Infinite Energy, awaken me to infinity even in the passage of time

58.

My mission in life is not merely
to survive, but to thrive;
and to do so with some passion,
some compassion,
some humor, and some style.

—MAYA ANGELOU

The autumn of life is bright and beautiful, a time of harvest in which the practices of a lifetime come to fruition. God wants us to have abundant life, now as much as always, a life filled with passion and compassion, with zest and flair. Abundance, liveliness, fullness of life: these were at the heart of Jesus' mission.

What does it mean for you to thrive? What harvests do you intend to gather in retirement? How might your thriving be a gift to the world? You are meant to be a light in the world, giving guidance and warmth. Your life is intended to be a blessing to others. Don't think small. Don't put your light under a bushel basket. Delight! Rejoice! Share! And above all, love!

Let the harvest of my life be bountiful, Spirit. Let my thriving bring joy to those around me.

59.

Keep alive the dream;
for as long as a person has a
dream in their heart,
they cannot lose the significance of living.

—HOWARD THURMAN

Dreams change. They grow and adapt along with our life circumstances. Sometimes they die, but other times they are resurrected. Our dreams always challenge us to be more than we can currently imagine. They lure us toward new pathways and possibilities. They beckon us to embrace new relationships or

new ways to embody previous relationships and professional activities. Without dreams, life loses luster.

What dreams are emerging in your life? What untapped possibilities energize you? Don't censor your imagination. Let your blueprints for castles in the air take form in daily life.

Loving Spirit, help me keep the dreams alive that call me forward into Your abundant life.

60.

One of the joys of retirement is
sitting on my back porch,
looking at the blue sky and wide vistas.
It restores my soul.

—DEBBIE HAY SANTOS, CLASS OF 1970

The Tao of retirement includes letting go of your agenda and simply taking in the vistas of creation—watching the river flow, gazing at scudding clouds, letting the planet revolve, and surrendering from your role as a god or goddess of your world, trying to be in control of the uncontrollable! Simply being

part of the vista expands our spirits and refreshes our souls. We gain spirits large enough to embrace far horizons with love and gratitude.

How might you find ways today to take in the world's vistas and restore your soul? What stands in your way?

Spirit, let me trust the forces of the universe
so that I might simply relax into beauty.
Let me embrace the amazing gift of this
moment, not having to do anything to prove my
worth.

61.

We wake up empty and frightened. . . .
Take down a musical instrument.
Let the beauty we love be what we do.
There are hundreds of ways to
kneel and kiss the ground.

—RUMI

We are made for beauty. We are made to rejoice in the wonders of life, to delight in art, music, poetry, and movement. And perhaps beauty is also an antidote to fear and emptiness. When we discover the abundant wellsprings of beauty and energy flowing

through us and around us, our problems fall into perspective. Beauty stills life's lamentations for a moment. Though we cannot deny—and must respond to—the injustices of life, threats to planetary survival, and our own aging process, how can we keep from singing, when beauty is everywhere?

How do you respond to the emptiness of life, the lamentations of the world? Where do you find beauty in your daily life? Let the beauty you love inspire you to greater compassion, creativity, Earth care, and justice-seeking?

Holy One, open my senses that I may discover the Beauty in whom I live and move and have my being.

62.

I'm going to have to slow down sometime.
But for now I'm out there every day,
meeting people and learning new things.

—GEORGE GARCIA, CLASS OF 1970

Better to flame out than rust out, so believes my classmate George Garcia. Having dealt with a variety of health issues, George greets each day with zest and gratitude. In his words, "Each morning when I wake up, I give thanks to the Grandfather and to the Sun for being alive." When there's life, there's not just hope, there's adventure, curiosity, and the never-ending quest to learn more about our wild and precious planet. How can life be boring when there are

so many sights to see, persons to meet, and projects to undertake? The only limits are those we place upon ourselves. We are in touch with the Sun and the Spirit in their infinity, and their infinity flows through us and energizes us. Every day can be an invitation to Narnia, a road to Damascus, a flight where none have gone before.

How do you greet the morning? What adventures await you? What new worlds do you wish to conquer? Your experience is unique, idiosyncratic, and amazing, if you simply open to the adventure on your front porch.

I thank You for sun, wind, and life, Great Spirit. Energize and inspire me to see each day as an adventure.

63.

Every moment is an organizing opportunity,
every person a potential activist,
every minute a chance to change the world.

—DOLORES HUERTA

One of the parents of the Farm Workers movement, seeking justice for the people who bring food to our tables, Dolores Huerta reminds us that we can experience joy through activism to transform the lives of the marginalized and mistreated. While holidays and hobbies contribute to a joyful retirement, so does working for a better world. Using our life experiences, our agency, and our organizational skills, we can help

to build the infrastructure for a healthy community, one where no one is left behind.

What community issues inspire you to activism? Where do your gifts and talents meet the needs of your community? Who can you join with to reach out to the marginalized and forgotten?

Spirit, help me use my gifts to transform my community and bring joy to children, fairness to the underrepresented, and justice to the marginalized. Let me become Your companion in healing the world.

64.

Your bliss can guide you to the
transcendent mystery,
because bliss is the welling up of the energy
of the transcendent wisdom within you....
The idea is to find your own pathway to bliss.

—JOSEPH CAMPBELL

A typo can say everything; in writing my first draft,
I typed "pathway to bless." Perhaps there is no
fundamental difference between blessing and blissing!
To bless and bliss involve moving from self-interest to
world loyalty. Joyful souls are large-spirited. Blissful
souls embody the spirit of Jesus and the Bodhisattva,

cultivate souls as large as the universe, embracing friend and foe alike. In letting go of their small souls, large-souled persons experience the Soul of the Universe. Retirement is an opportunity to discover the sage within, always waiting to come forth but hidden by our needs for security and recognition. Having lost our usual habits, professional status, and place in the pecking order, our world opens up; we become "mahatmas," great-souled persons, free to live and love, and delight in the bliss of the moment.

What is your personal bliss? What is your personal blessing for the world? What are the gifts of letting go of your small self to embrace a wider reality?

Let my life, Great Soul, be a blissful blessing to everyone I encounter.

65.

My story is a freedom song of struggle.
It is about finding one's purpose,
how to overcome fear and to stand up
for causes bigger than one's self.

—CORETTA SCOTT KING

Today's retirees cannot—at least initially—retire from the world. Future generations depend on us. We need to be the voices of courage, who cannot be bribed, coerced, or fired. We need to be willing to share our retirement with causes greater than ourselves, moving our attention from self-interest to world loyalty. We are called to be the elders and

grandparents of children we will never meet and generations we will never live to see. Retirement is a time to balance leisure pursuits with the pursuit of justice. As we expand, rather than contract, our sense of self, our souls grow in compassion, caring, and action to heal the earth and its peoples.

In your retirement, what great causes lure you forward? What issues tear you from self-interest to world loyalty? Where are you called to be a healer?

Grow my spirit, God, so that my spirit might join Yours in healing the Earth and its creatures.

66.

We are a multitude of individuals
within each of us—
manifestations of who we are
and who we could be—
and our challenge is to keep
them all in harmony.

—JOY KENNEDY-KUTAKA, CLASS OF 1970

Each of us has many selves, what psychologists sometimes call subpersonalities, often vying for attention or coming out of the blue to surprise us or create socially joyful or awkward situations. In retirement, certain aspects of our lives slow down, and we

have more time to experience the fullness of ourselves and experiment with undiscovered or marginalized parts of ourselves. Other parts, then, speed up as we explore alternative pathways toward the future. There is a hidden world in each of us, mysterious places in our souls and histories—helpful, awkward, joyful, painful, beautiful, and challenging—and the path to self-awareness is never-ending.

What hidden or deemphasized parts of yourself are you discovering? How might these aspects of yourself be either challenging or life-expanding? Rejoice in your complexity and find a home for your many selves, giving each its due so that they may come together in healthy and energetic ways, as guideposts for future adventures.

Divine Companion, I thank You for the wonder of my being.

67.

There is no such thing as to have one life to live.
The fact is that every life is a series of lives,
each one with its own task, its own flavor,
its own brand of errors, its own type of sins,
its own glories, its own kind
of deep, dank despair,
its own plethora of possibilities all designed
to lead us to the same end—
happiness and a sense of fulfillment.

—JOAN CHITTISTER

Each of us has many vocations, many purposes, that emerge in different environments, tasks, and ages. Every phase of our lives has its spiritual, intellectual, relational, experiential, and emotional potential and limits, and these are also the womb of possibility.

What losses have you experienced—or do you imagine—in retirement? Rejoice in uncertainty and welcome new paths as new vocations and images of yourself are born. Embrace this time of your life!

God of Infinite Creativity, let me build on the past new realms of possibility.

68.

We shall either extend or contract our activities;
but at all events we shall stir ourselves
and not be gripped and paralyzed by fear . . .
for self-preservation does not entail
suppressing oneself . . .
for the ultimate horror is to leave
the number of the living before you die.

—SENECA

Retirement brings a host of fears and provocative questions: Will I age well? Will I suffer from dementia? Will I matter to others? Can I still make

a difference? While certain life situations, as Seneca notes, may be out of our control, we still can be agents of our destiny and artists of our experiences. Our daily life can add beauty and healing to the world.

Where do you worry about not mattering? What shifts of focus and action will increase your sense of meaning and impact on the world? What beauty and joy can you share today? Be among the living! You matter!

Heart of the Universe, thank You for loving me, guiding me, and needing me.

69.

Love life. Engage in it. Give it all you've got.
Love it with a passion because
life truly gives back,
many times over, what you put into it.

—MAYA ANGELOU

A joyful retirement is the gift of intentionality and focus, grounded in the sense that life is a miracle. With all life's ups and downs, it is still beautiful and amazing. Poet Maya Angelou who faced many dangers, toils, and snares, is not asking us to do "one more thing" or stress out trying for one more experience. Instead, she is inviting us to live by our passions,

delight in the moment, and choose to make a differ-ence, embracing—not wasting—every season of life. Every moment can be a portal to the mystic. Every day is an invitation to adventure, every encounter a healing moment.

What do you love most about your life? What new passions call you forward? Be lofty in your thinking and elevate your spirit, recognize the amazing and intricate world in which we live. Embrace the wonder of the world and the wonder that is you.

Loving Spirit, fill me with passion and wonder as I seize each new day, giving fully and living completely.

70.

Just to be is a blessing.
Just to live is holy.

—ABRAHAM JOSHUA HESCHEL

During the pandemic, I often felt afraid. Each night I went to bed with a prayer for protection. Each morning I arose with a prayer of thanksgiving and a plea to make a difference in bringing God's realm to fruition, "on earth as it is in heaven." Post-pandemic, these are still my goals: to treasure life in its fragility, to be thankful for each breath, and to consecrate each day as a holy adventure in which God calls me to heal the world one encounter at a time.

Where do you experience blessing today? Where do you experience holiness? Retirement is a time of fruitage and blessing, a time to accept the life you have lived in all its ambiguity, joy, and sorrow, using your life in its maturity to bless others. Your life is holy. Your day is a sacrament. Your being is your gift to God.

God of all Creation, help me see holiness and be holiness. May each breath I take be a prayer and each act a blessing.

71.

The thing that I give thanks for each day
is that the values I taught my children stuck.
They are adults now and are
living meaningful lives.

—BRUCE BACON, CLASS OF 1970

The fruitage of retirement for many retirees involves deep relationships with the next generations. Sharing the values you have—and embodying them in day-to-day parenting and grandparenting—creates an intimate bond that cuts across generations. This bond is one of the blessings of retirement. Although it may sometimes require letting go of other aspects of our lives, love lasts forever, and the greatest love makes

sacrifice a joy and not a loss. Let us give thanks for the love in our lives and our role in shaping the next generations.

Who are the younger people in your life? What values have you shared with them? In the years ahead, what values will shape your relationship?

Spirit whose parenting embraces us all, may my love bear fruit in the unique creativity of future generations, helping to nurture values that bring joy and love to the world.

72.

Christ has no body now on earth but yours,
no hands but yours, no feet but yours.
Yours are the eyes through which to look out
as Christ's compassion to the world.
Yours are the feet with which he
is to go about doing good.
Yours are the hands through which
Christ is to bless people now.

—TERESA OF AVILA

Joyful retirement is also the result of loving and open-spirited intentionality as we remember that we are Divine agents and messengers, God's compan-

ions in healing the world. The Spanish mystic Teresa of Avila challenges us to commit ourselves to representing Christ in action: seeing Christ in others and being Christ to others. This means we go into every situation with the intention to bring God's love to the world, to advance God's cause in the world, and to move forward the moral and spiritual arcs of the universe. God needs us to be agents of healing, fostering social change as we address the challenges of our time with our unique sets of gifts and experiences. The work will be unfinished, but it will be meaningful and fulfilling!

Where do you see God needing your hands, feet, and heart?

Loving God, give me the energy and courage to be Your embodied love in the world.

73.

We must be willing to get rid of
the life we've planned,
so as to have the life that is waiting for us.

—JOSEPH CAMPBELL

Our retirement plans need to be flexible and subject to change. For example, I hadn't expected to retire in 2021, but the greater good of family commitments called me to leave my position and return to the Washington, DC, area. I had plans to retire on Cape Cod, delighting in sea, sky, pond, and sand, but now instead I will be navigating the complexities of the nation's capital. Still, in this change, new life awaits.

My wife and I will have brand-new adventures, challenges, responsibilities, and vocations. Right now, we can only see the horizons of the life to come. While there are no guarantees, I know there will be possibilities, and in them, we will find energy, delight, growth, and creativity.

What plans have you needed to let go of? Are you able to embrace the new, while giving thanks for the old? If not, what holds you back? As you release the life you had anticipated, you open the door new possibilities.

Give me the courage, Spirit, to embrace the unfolding future.

74.

The unexamined life is not worth living.

—SOCRATES

Retirement is a time of self-examination, of looking at your life, exploring your history and values, and then letting your life speak in acts of service and compassion. Often our professional lives had so many demands, not to mention the responsibilities of family and community, that our spiritual energy was sapped. So busy with our commitments, we often had little time to pause and reflect, to ask questions of meaning and purpose. Now, in our retirement years, we have time for reflection, introspection, prayer, and meditation.

At the end of each day, take time to reflect on the events of the past twenty-four hours, including moments of joy and sorrow, peace and anxiety, delight and boredom. When did you feel close to God? When did turn away from the Divine? Give thanks for the day, and then pray for God's guidance in the day to come. In pausing, noticing, and praying, we may discover a deeper rhythm and providence guiding our steps. We may claim new vocations for the years ahead.

Spirit of Love, remind me to take time for moments of reflection.

75.

**I will write about what it feels like
to be facing the time of life for
which there is no career path.**

—JOAN CHITTISTER

The words of Benedictine nun and spiritual guide Joan Chittister resonate with my experience. As I write this book in June 2021, for the first time in over forty years, I have no clear professional path mapped out. No classes planned. No congregation awaiting me. No consulting or preaching dates. While it is unsettling, it is also liberating as I ease into days without schedules. I do have visions for the future, but I have no agenda, nothing in my calendar other than

attending to my family responsibilities. Like the Celtic Christ-followers who set off on high seas without a rudder in search of their place of resurrection, the Divinely planned vision of their lives, I am opening my heart and mind to the holiness of an unplanned life—for a while! As I do so, I believe new paths will emerge and new adventures surface.

How do you feel about an unplanned life? What are the temptations and joys of a purposeless, rather than purpose-driven, day?

Spirit of both rest and activity, purpose and meandering, let me be open to going with the flow, changing course, and discovering the roads not previously traveled, knowing You are my Companion on every road.

76.

Sin happens when we refuse to keep growing.

—RICHARD ROHR

Persons who are fully alive are constantly growing. They embrace and own their past, learning from mistakes, redeeming failures, and building on accomplishments. They believe that today is a day of joyful service and tomorrow a day of adventure. They have open minds, and they are eager to learn new things, even if it means letting go of old ways of thinking. Every spiritual path is a source of wisdom

as they journey from their "home spirituality" to explore the wisdom of other traditions. Their hearts and minds range the universe, knowing that God encompasses all.

What horizons of learning beckon you forward?

God of growing things, let the forces of growth course through me. May I always look toward the horizons, living peacefully and yet restlessly in the quest to become fully alive.

77.

For the unlearned, old age is winter;
for the learned it is the season of harvest.

—THE TALMUD

The aging process brings a harvest, the fruit of a life well lived. There is a wintry spirit—the reality of loss, diminishment, and grief; letting go of our former images of ourselves; refocusing our identity when we have left behind the familiar projects that defined and bolstered our identities—but the harvest is here. This is a time of reaping loving relationships with life-companions, friends, children, and grandchildren. It is a time to appreciate the gifts of reflection, experience, and self-awareness. In this moment is eternity.

In the finite is Infinity. The seeds we've planted have matured into a harvest joyful wisdom.

Where do you experience a wintry spirit? What seeds of your earlier life are coming to fruition today? Which do you choose to focus on?

Let me age like good wine, Spirit. Let me burst forth from the winter of life with a harvest of love.

78.

Well, I didn't grow up with
that word "retirement"
as part of my consciousness.
I didn't grow up with professionals that retired.
I thought retiring was when you
are tired and go to bed.

—RUBY DEE

We may change the focus of our lives, work more
flexibly, and enjoy greater freedom, but retirement is not an invitation to sit on the sidelines watching life go by. Instead, freed from the pressures and
constraints of professional life, we may become more

like Ruby Dee, who remained an activist until her death at ninety-one. The world is full of opportunities for volunteering: food pantries and soup kitchens; homeless ministries; schools and hospitals; and organizations like Habitat for Humanity, Grandmothers Against Gun Violence, NAACP, and the American Civil Liberties Union. Retirement can mean sharing light rather than rusting out, becoming more involved in seeking God's realm on earth as it is in heaven.

What new ways of service inspire you? Where might the talents of your professional life be employed to support persons in your community?

Spirit of Transformation, inspire me to service, activism, and healing.

79.

I am grateful for waking up every morning.
I open the windows to the world, say my prayers,
and ask for wisdom and direction
to live each new day.

—ESTHER ALFEREZ HOGAN, CLASS OF 1970

Retirement can open us to a larger world, moving us away from tunnel vision to global vision. This phase of our life is an opportunity to shift from self-interest to world loyalty. In the process, as we discover our inner artist, writer, poet, or activist, some other aspect of ourselves that has lain dormant for decades, we discover we have something to contribute as citizens of the world rather than nine-to-five employees.

What larger vision motivates you? What do you notice now that you have more time on your hands? How will you respond? Open to the wider world. Let your soul expand. Let your interests range the planet and beyond.

Let my vision expand, Spirit, to embrace new ideas, strangers as well as friends, and unexplored parts of myself.

80.

In retirement many of us have the opportunity
to shuck unnecessary exoskeletons
and discover our true essence and radiance.

—VALERIE ZEHL

Sometimes we need to peel off the unnecessary self-images, professional personae, and self-imposed responsibilities to discover the deeper light within. Retirement is often a time for traveling light. For pruning all the branches, to use Jesus' imagery, that stifle the flowing energy of the vine. Simplifying your life—decluttering both your home and your spirit—may be painful, but from that spiritual and material subtraction come new freedom and greater energy for the next

steps of the journey. Lighter spirited, we discern more fully the light of God flowing in and through us.

What aspects of your "exoskeleton" do you need to peel off for a more joyful retirement? How might you dispense of the weight of a lifetime of your previous personae?

**Light of my life and Love of Creation,
give me the courage to peel away the inessential
to discover the deeper realities of my life.**

81.

It is not by muscle, speed, or physical dexterity
that great things are achieved
but by reflection, force of
character, and judgment.
In these qualities, old age is usually not poorer,
but is even richer.

—CICERO

I have had to let go of several things as I accept the aging process: I don't bound downstairs as my grandchildren do; instead, I hold onto the rail and place my feet carefully. I've given up long-distance running for long walks every morning. I'm more careful in my eating habits, and I must remember to take my medi-

cations each day. Still, the aging process has many benefits, if I take the time for self-discovery. My nearly seventy years of life experiences, when approached with wisdom and prayer, give me greater perspective, deliver me from the tyranny of the "urgent," and provide a wellspring of insight I can share with others. Aging is a time for grateful and graceful adventuring and service—and for that, I give thanks.

What gifts of aging do you celebrate? How might you use those gifts to help others?

Spirit, let me use the gifts of aging to be Your co-worker in healing the world.

82.

We are the only icons of aging that
young people will get to meet.
What we show them as we go,
gives them a model
for what they, too, can strive for.
We will show them the way to fullness of life.

—JOAN CHITTISTER

Each of us can be an icon—a portal to holiness—
for future generations. We can face life's necessary changes and losses with grace and dignity. We
can provide models of healthy generativity, of going
beyond self-interest to world loyalty. In many ways, we

chart the path that we hope they will live long enough to follow—joyful retirement, lifelong learning, zest for life, changing what we cannot accept and accepting what we cannot change, and finding holiness in our changed professional and health situation. In retirement and as we embrace the passage of time, let us be good ancestors whose lives provide guideposts for the adventures of future generations.

God of all seasons, let my life be an icon and model for future generations. Let my living be a gift to You, my contemporaries, and those who come after me.

83.

Grow old along with me!
The best is yet to be, the last of life,
for which the first was made.

—ROBERT BROWNING

In many ways, it's countercultural to think of retirement and aging as the best part of life, let alone the
best part of our relationships with significant others.
We are a youth-oriented culture, and aging persons
are often left behind. The assumption is that love
wanes, and passion dies as we age. Still, there is grace
and joy in long-term fidelity in which a couple share a
lifetime of memories, decisions, and common values,

as well as the familiar face and rituals, the history of parenting and grandparenting, and being there for one another in sickness and health, for better for worse, and for richer or poorer, knowing that love endures forever. Yes, the best is yet to come—the gentle fruit of a lifetime love.

What challenges have you encountered in your intimate relationship in retirement and aging? What are the unexpected joys? What practices nurture your relationship?

Spirit of Love, I thank You for the enduring joys of loving relationships.

84.

Spiritually speaking, there are no dead ends.

—RICHARD ROHR

God makes a way where we perceive no way, seeking the best possibilities for each moment of our lives. Even when we go astray or intentionally turn away, God still works for good in all things. This means that what we perceive to be dead ends are actually invitations to new pathways. Letting go of one path is often the beginning of a new adventure. The wall that apparently blocks our path challenges us to create a detour and go around or even leap over. In the walking, we will find our way even if there seems to be

no way forward, for God is our companion, opening the future and guiding us toward far horizons.

Where has a way been made where you believed no way was possible? Where has a failure been the foundation for a new adventure?

God of every pathway, help me find a way forward when all I see is a dead end. Open my senses to new routes and new possibilities and the wondrous horizon ahead for me.

85.

The world is hungering for volunteerism.
If we don't do it, it doesn't get done.

—HY LIBBY, CLASS OF 1970

A song from my teen years asks, "What are you doing with the rest of your life?" These words become especially provocative to persons heading into retirement. We may have the next third of our lives to look forward to, with reasonable health and energy for many years ahead. This phase of our lives offers opportunities for recreation, learning, and relationships. It also can open the door to new opportunities for volunteer work. When we connect our gifts and

time with the world's needs, the world is transformed one person and encounter at a time.

What forms of volunteerism inspire you? There are many ways to reach out to others. What skills and passions do you have that might match up with a need in your community?

Spirit of beloved community, join my spirit with all creation.

86.

**If you don't have a vision and clarity
on the destination you want to reach,
you'll simply never get there.**

—DEAN GRAZIOSI

Purpose is essential to the good life. When I served as a pastor of a Cape Cod church, one of my mantras was "I have a vision but not an agenda." A vision is the horizon that lures us forward, energizing our activities. In contrast, an agenda is a "have-to" we tell ourselves must be achieved. Life, however, is too complicated and has too many twists and turns for us to live by an inflexible agenda. Visions are the inspira-

tions and dreams that wake us up in the morning and motivate our actions. With a vision, we move forward creatively even on the most challenging days. We find fulfillment, despite setbacks, knowing we are part of a larger personal and planetary story.

What is your long-term vision? Has it changed since retirement? How is your vision lived out on a daily basis?

Artist of Creation and Poet of Possibility, let my vision emerge to bring joy and purpose to my life and beauty to the world.

87.

All children need a laptop. Not a
computer, but a human laptop.
Moms, dads, grannies and
grandpas, aunts, uncles—
someone to hold them, read to them, teach them.
Loved ones who will . . . pass on the experience,
rituals and knowledge of a hundred
previous generations.

—COLIN POWELL

Many grandparents and other older relatives become havens for the next generations. Our laps offer opportunities for learning the wisdom of the years. For some children, grandparents are the closest thing they'll encounter to "God with skin on." From us, they learn big and small things: what it means to have integrity and kindness, how to handle ordinary daily problems, and the rituals of our families and faith traditions.

In what ways do you pass your wisdom on to the next generation? What might the children in your life need to learn from you?

Grandparent Spirit, may I be Your Presence in children's lives, embodied in hugs and touches, smiles, and words of wisdom.

88.

Sad will be the day for every person
when they become contented
with the life they are living
and there is no longer some great
desire to do something larger
which they know that they were
meant and made to do.

—PHILLIPS BROOKS

Spirituality is about restlessness as well as contentment, energy as well as equanimity, and movement
as well as contemplation. As Ephesians 3:20 tells us,
God is able to do immeasurably more than we ask or

even imagine. Even in retirement, we can expect great things from ourselves and great things from God's energy of love coursing through our lives. A Divine discontent challenges us to aim high and claim our destiny as God's agents in the world. God tells us, "Don't think small. Remember that My dream for you is larger than you can ever imagine."

What large possibility lures you forward? How might you live out God's dream for you in your current life situation?

Spirit of Possibility, enlarge my vision.

89.

The purpose of life is not to be happy.
It is to be useful, to be honorable,
to be compassionate,
to have it make some difference that
you have lived and lived well.

—RALPH WALDO EMERSON

How countercultural Emerson's words are at first glance, and yet the Transcendentalist philosopher captures the essence of a good life and joyful retirement. I believe the world is transformed one day and moment at a time. Let us resolve as we wake each day

to ask God to help us bless everyone we meet, bringing beauty and love to every encounter.

Where does your life make a difference? In what ways might you be more attentive to God's vision for your life and your role in healing the world?

Loving God, let my life be a living witness that love is stronger than hate and that life triumphs over death.

90.

My core value is growth—
spiritual, emotional, psychological, relational.
There are a lot of possibilities of
life, to do things in the future.

—JOY KENNEDY KUTAKA, CLASS OF 1970

Jewish mysticism proclaims, "Every blade of grass has its Angel that bends over it and whispers, 'Grow, grow.'" The same holds true for us. An inner dynamic energy pushes us toward horizons of possibility. We have not finished our spiritual journeys, our emotional healing and transformations, our psychological discoveries, or our relational adventures. This

glorious day is the womb of possibility, and we are the midwives of the future.

What is yet to be born in your life? What possibilities for healing, growth, and adventure spur you on? With hope in your heart and a dream for tomorrow, each of your days can be filled with zest and adventure.

Spirit of constant transformation, help me to never stop growing.

91.

All that is dear to me
and everyone I love
are of the nature to change.
There is no way to escape
being separated from them.

—THICH NHAT HANH'S TRANSLATION OF
BUDDHISM'S FIVE REMEMBRANCES

All things flow. Or, as the Byrds, a group from my high school years, sing, echoing the wisdom of Ecclesiastes, "To everything turn, turn, turn, there is a season." There is a time for every season under heaven. All things flow, all things change—and so will my life. And yet, there is a steady thread that underlies

the constant change; as the hymn says, "My life goes on in endless song…how can I keep from singing." This *now*—this day that is different from any other that has gone before—is the day God has made, and I rejoice in gladness.

What changes do you fear in retirement? Can you imagine the gifts—the new worlds—that may emerge from these changes?

Spirit of time and change, when I fear the future, give me the courage to embrace the turning world with hope and agency.

92.

You will be enriched in every way
for your great generosity.

—2 CORINTHIANS 9:11

Generosity and generativity are joined in a joyful retirement. When we give to others, we become the recipients of greater energy and giftedness. Our spirits become more spacious and hospitable. We live by abundance. We have enough, and we are enough. When we give, we get back and, in the receiving, we have more to give to enrich future generations. When we enhance the well-being of our neighbors, we enrich God's life as well as our own. The beauty we share

with God and our neighbors flows back to us, inspiring us to greater acts of healing and enrichment. We become mahatmas, great-souled persons, whose love blesses everyone we meet.

Where are you being invited to share beauty with others?

Artist of the Universe, help me be Your beauty-giver, experiencing fulfillment even as I add to the joy of others.

93.

One of the greatest joys of my retirement
has been to finally and fully
know that I am enough—
and always have been.

—NANCY HARCOURT, COLLEGE CLASSMATE

Sometimes, we spend a lifetime thinking we are not up to a task, believing we need to measure up to some imaginary threshold, only to discover that we are already sufficient just as we are. Right now in this holy moment, we have everything we need to be fulfilled. We are sufficient. We may still grow and aspire to achieve our Great Work—but in the aspiration is the completion.

In what areas of your life have you believed you were inferior or lacking? Are you open to believing that God blessed you and approves of you, just as you are? Right now, in this Holy Here-and-Now, you are loved, you matter, and you can do something beautiful for God.

God of infinite love, thank You for the wonder of my being: my original wholeness, Your image within me.

94.

My vocation now is to pray.

—DOROTHY DAY

Sidelined by the diminishments that come with age, social activist Dorothy Day could no longer participate in public protests or give speeches—but she could still make a difference through her prayers. Prayer adds to the positive energy of life, surrounding those for whom we pray, opening new possibilities in their life. Prayer does not coerce God, nor can our prayers ensure that a specific outcome is achieved, but prayer connects our hearts with God's. What if ten million retirees in the USA committed to praying for

peace, civility, and justice—for the healing of the soul of the nation and the planet—on a daily basis? What if we prayed for greater wisdom and compassion among our world's leaders? What if we prayed for insight into how we can be agents in God's quest for a healed world? I believe the world would be transformed to more resemble God's vision of life "on earth as it is in heaven."

Could you consider making prayerfulness a part of your moment-by-moment response to life? Keep in mind that there are many ways to pray, and no single type of prayer is *the* way. What form of prayer works best for you?

Spirit of Love, may my every breath be a prayer.

95.

Wherefore we ought to fly away
from earth to heaven
as quickly as we can; and to fly
away is to become like God,
as far as this is possible; and
to become like God,
is to become holy, just, and wise.

—PLATO

A joyful retirement involves being both heavenly minded and earthly good: seeking to embody God's realm on earth as it is in heaven. The Holy One orders what would otherwise be chaotic, making pos-

sible the wonder of the heavens and the greatness of humankind. Our calling is to order our own personal cosmos, practicing spiritual cosmetology to bring beauty to our lives and the lives of others, as we recognize our inherent divinity.

What is your vocation as a divine representative at this time of your life? How might you see the grand picture of life more clearly, living by a vision of truth, beauty, and goodness, and then letting these values flow into your daily life?

God of both order and chaos, let my life be aligned with Your vision of truth, beauty, and goodness.

96.

There is no fear in love,
but perfect love drives out all fear.

—JOHN 4:18

As we enter the pilgrimage of retirement, many of us have fears and anxieties. We wonder if we will be consigned to life's sidelines. Will we find meaning and purpose? What will fill our days? Will we matter to others—or be a nuisance? Will life pass us by? Will we experience physical diminishment, dementia, and disability? Fear is not final, though, and we need not be paralyzed by our worst nightmares. Love is the answer to our fear: love that joins us with others, love

that inspires sacrifice, love that takes us beyond self-interest to world loyalty, love that sees our lives intimately connected with all creation, love that inspires us to do something beautiful for God and for our decedents.

At this point in your life, what do you fear most? How do your experiences of love bring peace and meaning to you?

Spirit whose love spins forth galaxies and the human adventure, let love be my goal and purpose today.

97.

Look to this day: For it is life,
the very life of life. . . .
Today well-lived, makes yesterday
a dream of happiness
and every tomorrow a vision of hope.
Look well therefore to this day;
such is the salutation to the ever-new dawn!

—KALIDASA

Emerging from eternity and stretching into infinity, this moment is the womb of possibility and wonder. On this unrepeatable day, I have life and breath and love. No day is like today. No moment like this

moment. Regardless of the past, in this moment, I can choose love and beauty. I can begin again. I can be born again. I can live.

What unique gift are you receiving today? What unique gift can you share today? What new possibility can you give birth to today? You woke up this morning—now let the adventures begin!

**God of each moment and all Eternity,
thank you for today and all that it will bring.**

98.

This is the day that God has made,
let us rejoice and be glad in it.

—PSALM 118:24

How you begin each day is crucial. Will today be dominated by scarcity thinking, regret, and anxiety? Or will today be filled with adventures and possibilities? Sometimes, however, the reality of depression due to trauma or medical reasons may cloud our lives, and no act of will is able to deliver us. Medication, therapy, and spiritual direction can restore our sense of well-being—and we can reclaim agency for our personal lives, choosing gratitude and creativity even

when confronted with life's challenges. Life is larger than the crises we face. Even in tragedy, we may discover beauty, compassion, and faith.

What activities give you joy? What are the challenges that cloud your joy? How can you be a joy giver?

Give me grace to rejoice in this day, Spirit.
May I bring joy to those around me.

99.

If I am not for myself, who will be for me?
If I am only for myself, what am I?
And if not now, when?

—HILLEL THE ELDER

An older contemporary of Jesus (he died when Jesus was a child), Hillel captures the two pieces of Jesus' counsel to love your neighbor *as yourself.* Given the realities of agism that often attend retirement, we may have to become advocates for ourselves and our significant others. We need to love ourselves enough to ensure the best future possible. And all the while, self-love and self-interest needs to be balanced

by world loyalty and advocacy for others. As the days of our lives stretch from autumn into winter, we need to claim life—now! There is no time to defer joy. No reason to withhold words of love and acts of kindness. This is the day of salvation and healing! Now is the time for love!

Where do you need to advocate for yourself? Where are you challenged to advocate for others?

Heart of the Universe, let my heart beat with love for myself and all creation.

100.

Praised be You, my Lord,
through our Sister Bodily Death,
from whom no living man can escape.

—FRANCIS OF ASSISI

Why would anyone praise death? If we love this lifetime, isn't death an affront to our hopes, dreams, and loves? And yet the saint of Assisi sees death also as a blessing and revelation of God's loving providence. I must admit that I struggle to be as affirmative about death as Francis. I wonder about the great "what's next?" I also worry about the dying process itself. Will I still be able to be an agent of my own destiny, or

will I be rendered passive by pain or dementia? Will I go gentle into the night or rage against the inevitable? Will I accept the reality of death or grieve the loss of relationships? Francis of Assisi believed that nothing can separate us from the love of God, not even death. The one who loved us into life will receive us with loving arms at the moment of our deaths. We are in God's care now and forever more. Thanks be to God!

What are your feelings about death? How might the confidence that God's love never ends transform your attitudes toward death?

Eternal and Everlasting God, help me to trust You in life and death.

101.

Nothing that is worth doing can
be achieved in our lifetime;
therefore we must be saved by hope. . . .
Nothing we do, however virtuous,
can be accomplished alone;
therefore we must be saved by love . . .
[and] the final form of love which is forgiveness.

—REINHOLD NIEBUHR

Every life is partial, imperfect, finite, and incomplete. No task is ever finished. In retirement, as we are called to live boldly, we are also invited to receive grace for our imperfections. We recognize we are complicit in injustice, and that our carbon footprint

and the national debt we've left for future generations is greater than we can imagine. Our enlightenment sheds light on life's joy and divinity, but it also reveals our fallibility and bias. A joyful retirement requires accepting daily graces—the help of others, forgiveness when we thought we were right but weren't, and hope from greater wisdom when we have lost our path. That is the heart of a joyful retirement: living each day with gratitude, trust, and a compassionate heart, as we awaken to the wonder of this never-ending journey. *Thank you! Thank you! Thank you!*

Where do you need to reach out for help? Where do you need to acknowledge error and accept forgiveness?

With beauty and love all around me, Spirit, let me never cease to love.

101 Soul Seeds

for Peacemakers & Justice Seekers

Authentic spirituality embeds us in the pain of the world and inspires commitment to social justice and conflict resolution. It seeks peace and justice in the public sphere, while nurturing a sense of connection with both God and all creation. Rooted in the deep mystery of Divine love, we can face challenges with confidence that God's vision of justice and peace will outlast the demagogues, dictators, and destroyers.

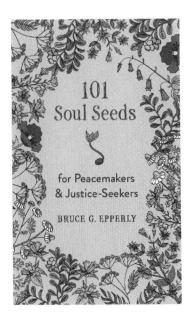

This book is intended to support your integration of peacemaking, justice-seeking, and spiritual growth.

Paperback Price:
$12.99

Kindle Price:
$4.99

101 Soul Seeds

for Parents of Adult Children

Being a parent held joys and challenges every step of the way, and never more so than when our children finally made it to adulthood. Now we can connect with them on deeper levels than ever—but unexpected potential pitfalls dot this new path we're traveling. *101 Soul Seeds for Parents of Adult Children* offers observations and quotes, coupled with simple prayers to help us navigate this portion of parenting . . . so we and our adult children grow closer to one another and closer to our own souls' destination.

Paperback Price: $12.99

Kindle Price: $4.99

101 Soul Seeds

for Grandparents Working for a Better World

Grandparenting is truly a holy adventure. As we see and bring forth the inner divinity of our grandchildren, we have the opportunity to show them that they are not only our beloved grandchildren but God's children as well, infinite in worth and possibility.

This book is an invitation to consider grandparenting as a spiritual and ethical vocation. As

we commit ourselves to love and pray for our grandchildren, we can also work to create a just and healthy world for all grandchildren.

Paperback Price:
$12.99

Kindle Price:
$4.99

Anamchara Books

www.AnamcharaBooks.com

Made in the USA
Middletown, DE
08 November 2022

14288531R00135